W9-BUE-887

101 Reasons
Why a Cat Is Better
than a Man

Allia Zobel

Illustrations by Nicole Hollander

BOB ADAMS, INC.
Holbrook, Massachusetts

Text copyright ©1994 Allia Zobel.
Illustrations copyright ©1994 Nicole Hollander.
All rights reserved, including the right to
reproduce this book or portions thereof in any
form whatsoever. For information contact
Bob Adams, Inc., 260 Center Street
Holbrook, Massachusetts 02343.

ISBN: 1-55850-436-2

C D E F G H I J

Printed in Korea.

Cover design by Tom Greensfelder.

This book is available at quantity discounts for bulk purchases.
For information call 1-800-872-5627.

For my parents, Alvin and Lucille; my feline-like mate, Desmond Finbarr Nolan, and the cats who helped me write this book: Oscar, Pookie, Twinkle-Toes Nose, Scruffy, Vanessa, and Winston-Stanley III ("the thoid").

—A.Z.

I'd like to dedicate this book to my feline companions Buddy and Izzy for their invaluable help in drawing the illustrations for this book, and I humbly apologize if I was less respectful to them about anything at any time.

—N.H.

With special thanks to my editor, Brandon Toropov,
and the rest of the Bob Adams gang for believing in me.

—A.Z.

Introduction

I HAVE NOT ALWAYS had a man in my life, but I have
always had a cat. Whether it was Oscar, Pookie,
Twinkle-Toes Nose, Scruffy, Winston-Stanley III, or
Vanessa, each cat possessed a very special attribute
that demonstrated his or her abundant intelligence and
inimitable sensitivity. They all adored me.

What do these four-legged creatures have that their
two-legged counterparts don't? Call it a sixth sense, or
call it a penchant for true creature comfort. Whatever it
is, it makes for a lasting, joyous relationship. Still, I'm
not advocating giving up on men altogether. I'm just
suggesting that women be more selective by looking for
someone who's warm, playful, loving, affectionate,
trustworthy, and patient. Someone who thinks you're

the greatest and accepts you "as is." Someone who'd sit alongside the tub and keep you company while you bathe.

Someone, in short, a lot like a cat. Enjoy!

ALLIA ZOBEL

Cats love when you fuss over them.

Cats are not afraid of commitment.

Cats don't believe in divorce.

A CAT THINKS YOU SHOULD HAVE LOTS OF SHOES.

A CAT DOESN'T CARE HOW YOU
LOOK IN THE MORNING.

A cat would never flirt with your friends.

A cat would never tell you how to dress or grouse that you wear too much makeup.

Though they're impeccable about grooming, cats don't hog the bathroom.

CATS DON'T LEAVE the toilet SEAT UP.

CATs love to listen to you SING.

Cats are never sarcastic.

A cat would never use *your* razor
for his face.

A cat would never bet on the horses.

Cats are loyal. They don't give their affection to just anyone who strokes them.

A CAT WOULD NEVER HOG THE REMOTE.

A cat would just as soon curl up with a good book, or play with a yarn mouse, as watch trash TV.

Cats are easy to live with.

Cats love to cuddle.

CATS LOWER YOUR BLOOD PRESSURE.

CATS THINK YOU LOOK SMART
IN GLASSES.

Cats are great company.

Cats adore independent women.

Cats don't worry about being
politically correct.

A cat would never apologize to
his friends because you're
a vegetarian.

A CAT WOULD NEVER HANG A MOOSE HEAD
IN THE LIVING ROOM.

Cats don't hold a grudge.

Cats are civilized.

A cat doesn't need a Rottweiler to make him feel macho.

A cat doesn't need to be right 100 percent of the time.

A cat doesn't care if you beat him at Jeopardy.

Cats like to exercise with you.

CATS LOVE TO PUTTER IN THE GARDEN.

A cat doesn't need to go out in
the woods with other cats,
beat drums, light fires,
and dance to get in touch
with his cathood.

A cat isn't threatened if you have
a lot of friends.

A cat would never ask you to sign
a palimony agreement.

Cats aren't afraid to be vulnerable.

cats are patient.

CATS REGULARLY BRING YOU TOKENS OF THEIR AFFECTION.

Cleavage doesn't interest a cat unless it's big enough to sleep in.

Cats listen when you talk about your day.

Cats don't exaggerate the truth.

CATS BELieve iN the SiMPLE PLEASures.

CATS DON'T CARE IF YOUR HOUSEKEEPING
IS LESS THAN PERFECT.

You can kiss a cat all night and never get razor burn.

You never have to entertain your cat's boss.

Cats don't borrow money.

A cat would never finish
your sentences.

A CAT WOULD NEVER GRILL YOU ABOUT
OTHER CATS YOU'VE KNOWN.. ALMOST NEVER.

CATS COMPREHEND the IMPORTANCE
OF BEING AFFECTIONATE.

A cat will wait and rub up against your legs no matter what time you get home.

You can talk all night on the phone and a cat will never give you the evil eye.

You never feel alone when you're with a cat.

CATS NEVER COMPLAIN ABOUT YOUR MOTHER.

A CAT MIGHT WEAR A WIG, BUT NEVER A toupee.

Cats understand how difficult
it is to keep your nails looking good
and what a disaster it is if you
break one.

Cats know good grooming
takes time.

Cats don't make jokes at your expense.

CATS LIKE TO HEAR THE SAME STORY OVER AND OVER AGAIN.

CATS DON'T CARE WHAT COLOR YOUR HAIR IS OR WHETHER IT'S SHORT OR LONG.

Rich, slim, or witty you needn't be.
A cat will love you unconditionally.

A cat would never tell you you look
better in high heels.

Cats are not intimidated by your accomplishments.

Cats don't engage in power plays.

CATS MISS YOU WHEN YOU GO ON A BUSINESS trip.

CATS ARE interested in WHAT YOU're
interested in.

Cats give you honest feedback.
They don't believe in patronizing,
especially when it comes to
your work.

Cats don't have beer bellies.

You'll never hear a cat burp
at the table.

Cats don't pick their teeth
with matchbook covers.

A CAT WOULD NEVER SMOKE
A CIGAR IN THE DINING ROOM.

A cat won't have a hemorrhage
if you wreck your car.

A cat is never too busy to take
a vacation.

Cats don't think daydreaming is
a waste of time.

CATS KNOW HOW IMPORTANT NAPS ARE.

CATS APPLAUD ALL YOUR DECISIONS.

Cats don't get annoyed if you snap your gum.

Cats don't care if you're older than they are.

Cats don't tell you what to do.

A cat would never ask you to have
"his" litter.

Cats don't keep secret bank accounts.

CATS NEVER COMPLAIN IF THEIR
DINNER COMES OUT OF A CAN.

Cats know when they've had enough to drink.

A cat would never walk around with food on his whiskers.

Cats don't hog the sheets
and could care less if you slather
yourself with cold cream.

A cat would never ask you to
wear anything to bed that would
make Howard Stern blush.

CATS DON'T MIND IF YOU SNORE.

cats take time to smell the flowers.

Cats don't need high-tech toys—
a grocery bag will do.

A cat would never give your number to another cat without telling you.

A cat would never take advantage of you if you had too much to drink.

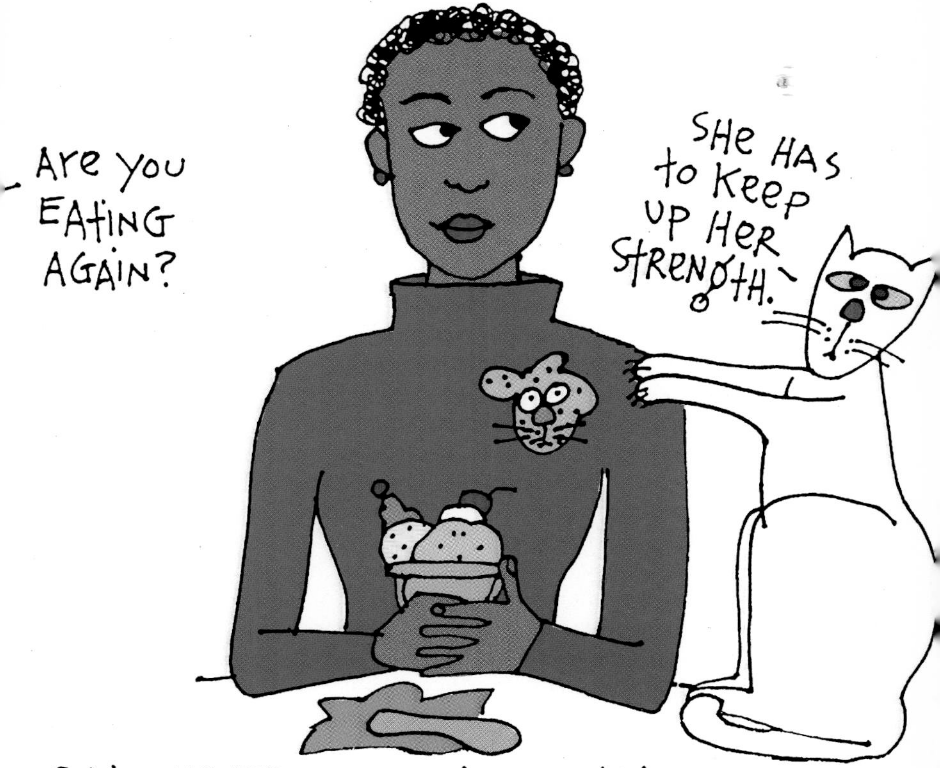

CAts NeveR MAKe insensitive ReMARKs IF you Go OFF your diet.

A CAT is NEVER EMBARRASSED WHEN YOU TALK BABY TALK TO HIM.

A cat appreciates when you cook
him something special.

Cats love quiet, intimate dinners.

Cats realize you're only human.

Cats (k)need you.

CATS LOOK FORWARD to GROWING OLD WiTH YOU.

About the Author

Allia Zobel is the author of *The Joy of Being Single* and *Younger Men Are Better than Retin-A*. She lives in Bridgeport, Connecticut. After spending much of her adulthood living happily with cats, she has recently wed, and is currently conducting field research on life with both men and cats.

About the Illustrator

Nicole Hollander's nationally syndicated comic strip *Sylvia* has a devoted following from coast to coast. Ms. Hollander lives in Chicago, Illinois.

What's your reason why a cat is better than a man?
Write it down and send it to the authors care of:

Bob Adams, Inc.
260 Center Street
Holbrook, Massachusetts 02343

If we use it in a future book, we'll credit you. All
responses become the property of Bob Adams, Inc.